20TH CENTURY MUSIC

1960s
AGE OF ROCK

Malcolm Hayes

Heinemann
LIBRARY

CONTENTS

CHANGING TIMES
*In the Sixties, the singer-songwriter in
rock music became something more
than an entertainer. Bob Dylan's songs
and performances had a tough,
cutting edge as they protested against
the restrictions and injustices of war
and conventional society.*

ALTERNATIVE LIFESTYLE
*The hippie way of life blended
escapism with rebellion. It involved
'dropping out' of the social and
financial obligations of capitalist
society and 'turning on' instead to
different values, including those
of rock music.*

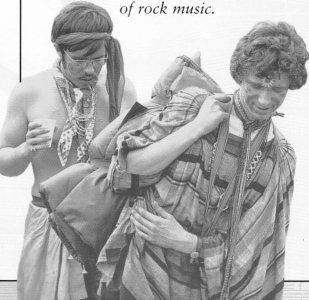

20TH CENTURY MUSIC
1960s
AGE OF ROCK

20TH CENTURY MUSIC – 1960s
was produced by

David West ⚈⚈ Children's Books
7 Princeton Court
55 Felsham Road
London SW15 1AZ

Picture Research: Carrie Haines
Designer: Rob Shone
Editor: James Pickering

First published in Great Britain in 2001 by
Heinemann Library, Halley Court, Jordan Hill,
Oxford OX2 8EJ, a division of Reed Educational and
Professional Publishing Limited.

OXFORD MELBOURNE AUCKLAND
JOHANNESBURG BLANTYRE GABORONE
IBADAN PORTSMOUTH (NH) USA CHICAGO

05 04 03 02 01
10 9 8 7 6 5 4 3 2 1

ISBN 0 431 14213 0 (HB)
ISBN 0 431 14220 3 (PB)

British Library Cataloguing in Publication Data

Hayes, Malcolm
The 60s: age of rock. - (20th century music)
1. Music - 20th century - Juvenile literature
I. Title II. Nineteen sixties
780.9'04

Printed and bound in Italy

PHOTO CREDITS :
Abbreviations: t-top, m-middle, b-bottom, r-right,
l-left.

Front cover m - Popperfoto, br - (Martin Langer)
Redferns. 4t, 5m & 16t, 10m, 16b, 17 all, 19bl & br,
20bl, 22b, 23ml (Michael Ochs Archive), 3 & 15tl,
13tr & br, 18tr, 22tr, 23tr (David Redfern), 10-11b
(Chuck Boyd), 7t (Martin Langer), 10t (Astrid
Kirchherr), 12bl (S&G Press Agency), 12-13m (Glenn
A. Baker), 13tl, 14ml (Val Wilmer), 14b (Dick
Barnata), 14t (Robert Johnson), 15b (Chuck Stewart),
18b (Gai Terrell), 19mt (Keith Morris), 21ml (Elliott
Landy), 21mb (Herb Green), 23br (Andrew Putler),
25br (David Farrell), 20tr (WHO:RB6919), 11tl -
Redferns. 7mr, 9br, 25tr, 26bl, 27tm, 29ml & br -
Lebrecht Collection. 6-7b, 27b - Andre
LeCoz/Lebrecht Collection. 8tr - David
Farrell/Lebrecht Collection. 8b - G.
MacDomnic/Lebrecht Collection. 9t - Mike
Evans/Lebrecht Collection. 9mr - B. Freeman/Lebrecht
Collection. 5tr & 24tr, 25bl - Milein Cosman/Lebrecht
Collection. 29tl - Greg Tomin/Lebrecht Collection. 4b,
5b, 10bl - Popperfoto. 21tr, 26mr, 28tr & bl - Hulton
Getty. 6m, 11br - Rex Features. 24bl - Photo - Alex
Sobolewski.

*Front cover: The Beatles (main image), Karlheinz
Stockhausen.*

*The dates in brackets after a person's name
give the years that he or she lived.*

*An explanation of difficult words can be
found in the glossary on page 30.*

ALL YOU NEED – WELL, ALMOST ALL – IS LOVE

For most of the developed western world, the Sixties were a time of economic prosperity. The communist-led governments in the Soviet Union and eastern Europe continued to suppress individual cultural freedoms, supposedly for the greater good of society as a whole. Meanwhile those same freedoms flourished under the capitalism of the increasingly prosperous west.

'Freedom' of any kind – to enjoy yourself, to make choices, to protest, to travel – is much more possible when you have some money in your pocket. The war in the divided south-east Asian state of Vietnam, with the North backed by the Soviet Union and the South by the United States (with its own GI troops), became a focus of this mood of rebellion against authority – a mood spurred on by a deep desire to break with the social conventions of the past. And the arrival of a brilliant new generation of rock musicians meant that popular music became identified with this dream of a new and more truly 'free' world.

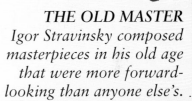

THE OLD MASTER
Igor Stravinsky composed masterpieces in his old age that were more forward-looking than anyone else's.

CHART-TOPPERS
Led by Diana Ross (centre), the Supremes were the most successful female vocal group of the Sixties. Ross later went solo.

MEGASTARS
The sensationally successful Beatles each received an MBE medal from the Queen in 1965.

5

EUROPE: TRADITION AND ADVENTURE

From now on, classical music was about the reality that 'anything goes'. A huge and confusing network of ancient and modern styles and techniques was to hand. Perhaps more so even than before, only powerfully gifted individuals could succeed.

MESSIAEN: THE MASTER AT WORK

France's Olivier Messiaen (1908–92) matched the younger generation's adventurousness while remaining true to his two great inspirations, the Catholic faith and the world of nature. The awesome grandeur of *Et Exspecto Resurrectionem Mortuorum* (And I Await the Resurrection of the Dead, 1964) was inspired by the biblical Book of Revelation. In 1969, Messiaen completed his vast, ten-movement oratorio *La Transfiguration de Notre-Seigneur Jésus-Christ*.

CHANCE AND CHOICE

Pierre Boulez (born 1925) became increasingly important as a conductor, while continuing also to compose. His main project was *Pli selon Pli* (Fold on Fold, 1962, with later revisions). This was a hugely complicated orchestral work involving 'aleatory' or 'chance' techniques. Jean Barraqué (1928–73) explored a rather different musical idiom – radical in tone, but broader and more spacious – in *Chant après Chant* (Song after Song, 1966) and his Clarinet Concerto (1968).

MUSIC THAT SPECULATES
Karlheinz Stockhausen (born 1928) created avant-garde music close to the spirit of the rock era. *Kontakte* (Contacts, 1960) for piano, percussion and electronic tape, is a Sixties classic, as is *Stimmung* (Tuning and/or Mood, 1968). Stockhausen knew Paul McCartney (pp. 10–11), and his ideas may have partly influenced the Beatles' later albums, including *Sergeant Pepper's Lonely Hearts Club Band* (1967).

FATHER FIGURE
Messiaen's music had a powerful following among composers and listeners alike.

6

Stockhausen's works often involved suggestions for improvised performance rather than actual musical notes.

NEW SOUNDS
György Ligeti settled in Vienna, where his music explored new and often beautiful possibilities of the collective sound of instruments playing together.

LEADING FROM THE FRONT
Pierre Boulez put over his radical musical views both in his own compositions and in his increasingly high-profile work as an international conductor. Here he rehearses Stravinsky's The Rite of Spring *in 1963.*

OPERA AND OTHER EXPERIMENTS

Die Soldaten (The Soldiers, 1960), by Germany's Bernd Alois Zimmermann (1918–70), is a bleak story of the corrupting effect of militarism on the human spirit. It involves complex staging and image-projection on to multiple screens. Hungarian exile György Ligeti (born 1923) composed music where melody and harmony blend in rippling tapestries of sound, as in his orchestral *Atmosphères* (1961) and *Lontano* (Distant, 1967) and choral *Requiem* (1965). Ligeti also explored a far-out kind of sound-theatre in *Aventures* and *Nouvelles Aventures* (Adventures and New Adventures, 1966). The music of Iannis Xenakis (1922–2001) blended complicated mathematical processes with eruptive power. His major statements included the fiendishly difficult *Eonta* (Being, 1964) for piano and brass and *Nuits* (Nights, 1968) for unaccompanied chorus.

ENGLAND: BRITTEN TO BIRTWISTLE

Britain is both a part of the continent of Europe and an island nation on its rim. True to form, English composers took notice of musical developments in mainland Europe, while continuing to go their own, often rather different way.

AT HOME IN SUFFOLK

Benjamin Britten (1913–76) planned and directed the Aldeburgh Festival on the Suffolk coast where he lived, while composing as fluently as ever. His operas included *A Midsummer Night's Dream* (1960) and a set of three *Church Parables* (1964–68). *War Requiem* (1961) was an oratorio with a remarkable difference. Besides the Latin words of the Requiem Mass, Britten included poems by Wilfred Owen, who served and died in the First World War.

DIFFERENT DIRECTIONS

Michael Tippett (1905–98) explored harder-edged territory than he had before in *King Priam* (1961), an opera based on the Ancient Greek poem of the Trojan War, Homer's *Iliad*. Malcolm Arnold (born 1921), famous as a film composer, continued a fine cycle of symphonies with his Fourth and Fifth (both 1960) (see also p. 21). Catalan exile Roberto Gerhard (1896–1970) wrote his brilliant Concerto for Orchestra (1965) and his chamber works *Libra* (1968) and *Leo* (1969).

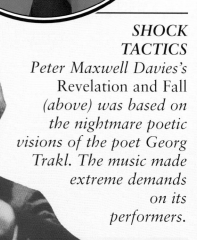

SHOCK TACTICS
Peter Maxwell Davies's Revelation and Fall (above) was based on the nightmare poetic visions of the poet Georg Trakl. The music made extreme demands on its performers.

BRITTEN
Pictured here conducting at the London Proms (Promenade Concerts), Britten was firmly established as his country's leading classical composer. He was also a superlative pianist, and often played chamber music at the Aldeburgh Festival.

A TRUE RADICAL

Harrison Birtwistle (below) achieved the uncompromising, startlingly original sound of works such as Tragoedia, Punch and Judy *and* Verses for Ensembles (1969) *by combining a hard-edged, avant-garde style with techniques adapted from medieval classical music.*

TIPPETT'S STAR RISES – AT LAST

Michael Tippett's visionary, mystical opera The Midsummer Marriage *(1955) was little understood or appreciated until its production at London's Royal Opera House (above) in 1969. The huge success of that staging and its recording helped to make Tippett internationally famous.*

THE NEW GENERATION: FASTEN YOUR SEAT BELTS

Peter Maxwell Davies (born 1934) ferociously developed Schoenberg's atonal style in *Revelation and Fall* (1966) – where a nun in a scarlet costume at one point screams through a megaphone – and in his orchestral *Worldes Blis* (World's Bliss, 1969). And Harrison Birtwistle (born 1934) outraged and impressed audiences with extremes of stridency and lyricism in *Tragoedia* (1965) for chamber orchestra, and in his opera *Punch and Judy* (1968).

IN ITALY

William Walton (1902–83) settled on the Italian island of Ischia. The tone of his later music was subtler and more refined than that of his earlier works. Besides two masterly creations, a Second Symphony (1960) and the *Variations on a Theme by Hindemith* (1963), Walton completed a witty one-act opera, *The Bear* (1967).

The Aragonese Castle off the island of Ischia

THE BEATLES: FROM MOPTOP TO PSYCHEDELIA

STARTING OUT
The first Beatles line-up in Hamburg, 1960, including Pete Best (far left) and Stu Sutcliffe (far right)

In July 1957 a very young singer and guitarist from Liverpool, Paul McCartney (born 1942), met another, John Lennon (1940–80). Within three years they had become the nucleus of the Beatles. The story of the most talented and successful pop group of all time had begun.

THE PRODUCER
George Martin (second from right), the Beatles' highly imaginative recording producer, pictured with (from left) McCartney, Harrison, Starr and Lennon.

EARLY DAYS

By 1960, Lennon and McCartney had been joined by lead guitarist George Harrison (born 1943), bass guitarist Stu Sutcliffe and drummer Pete Best. The group spent a lot of time in Hamburg, where Sutcliffe left: McCartney soon switched to bass guitar. Back in England, Ringo Starr (born Richard Starkey, 1940) took over on drums in 1962.

THE MANAGER
Brian Epstein (far left) with the group on Ed Sullivan's television show in America, 1964. The Beatles never really recovered from the shock of Epstein's death in 1967.

Peter Blake's cover photograph of Sergeant Pepper assembled many of the Beatles' heroes in an elaborate montage.

1967: THE PINNACLE

By mid-1967, the Beatles had stopped touring. There had been death threats, and besides, they couldn't hear themselves above the audience's screaming. The album *Sergeant Pepper's Lonely Hearts Club Band* was put together entirely in the recording studio at Abbey Road, London. Songs as different as 'Lucy in the Sky with Diamonds', 'When I'm Sixty Four' and 'A Day in the Life' (complete with symphony orchestra) set an immortal standard.

ULTIMATE TALENT, ULTIMATE FAME

By April 1964, Beatlemania had swept Britain and Europe, and the 'Fab Four' also had five singles at the top of the US charts. Lennon and McCartney (and sometimes Harrison) were now writing almost all the Beatles' own songs – a new development for a pop group. Lennon provided their music's cutting edge, while McCartney drew together the influences of rock, pop, and his own brand of gentle ballad. A host of huge hits ranged from the early singles 'From Me to You' and 'Can't Buy Me Love' to the albums *Please Please Me* (1963), *Beatles for Sale* (1964), *Help!* (1965, including 'Yesterday') and the boldly adventurous *Revolver* (1966). There were also two films: *A Hard Day's Night* (1964) and *Help!* (1965).

11

JOHN AND PAUL DURING THEIR FINAL TOUR
McCartney (left: he plays the bass guitar left-handed) and Lennon were two very different songwriting talents who sometimes argued fiercely, but also struck brilliant sparks off each other's creativity.

FINAL CHAPTER

After the creation of *Sergeant Pepper*, the group was destabilized by quarrels and walkouts. But before the Beatles disbanded in April 1970 they managed to record a double 'White Album' (1968, released in a plain white cover) and two superb single albums, *Abbey Road* (1969) and *Let It Be* (1970).

END OF AN ERA
One of the last pictures taken of the 'Fab Four' together, at the house of John Lennon (left) in 1969.

ENGLAND ROCKS AMERICA

The Beatles' massive success in America from 1964 onwards was a landmark in popular music. So far, the story of the 20th century had been about the impact of American music – blues, jazz and Elvis Presley – on Europe. Now the tide was flowing the other way.

A SPECIAL CITY

Much of the Sixties rock era had its roots in Liverpool. The city on the River Mersey has a different character from others in Britain – more freewheeling and cosmopolitan, with a large Irish community, many of whom have links with America (many Liverpudlians have emigrated there). Merseyside groups like Gerry and the Pacemakers were making the transition from Fifties rock 'n' roll to Sixties pop before the Beatles came along. Cilla Black, also from Liverpool, was famous as a singer before her career as a television presenter took over.

BLAZING THE TRAIL
Gerry and the Pacemakers (below) were the first group in the British charts to achieve three No. 1 hits with their first three singles. They are pictured here at Liverpool's Cavern Club, where the Beatles also often appeared.

THE STONES ARRIVE

Formed in London in 1962, the Rolling Stones dominated Sixties rock 'n' roll almost as completely as the Beatles were the giants of pop-rock. Fusing rock and blues in their own provocative way, the Stones scored a huge hit in Britain and America with '(I Can't Get No) Satisfaction' (1965). Keith Richards's guitar-playing, Mick Jagger's aggressive vocals and Charlie Watts's tight drumming are still at the heart of the group's superstardom.

The Rolling Stones:
(from left) Charlie Watts, Bill Wyman, Brian Jones, Keith Richards, Mick Jagger

12

BRITISH POP TAKES OFF

The Beatles' sensational success paved the way for other groups who would be bigger names, had the Fab Four not so dominated the early Sixties. The Dave Clark Five notched up a number of hits. So did Manfred Mann (whose band included Jack Bruce, p. 15), the Hollies and Herman's Hermits.

MANFRED MANN
Mann (far left) led his group from the keyboard, while Paul Jones (centre) supplied the vocals.

13

AMONG THE BEST: THE ANIMALS

The Animals started out in Newcastle in 1962, with a line-up centred around lead vocalist Eric Burdon and Alan Price on keyboards. That year their version of the traditional ballad 'The House of the Rising Sun' topped the singles charts in Britain and America. It was followed by more hit singles, worldwide tours and a sequence of albums: *The Animals* (1964), *Animal Tracks* (1965) and *Animalism* (1966). For a time the group's bass guitarist was Chas Chandler (see Jimi Hendrix, p. 15).

THE ANIMALS
Appearing on the television show Ready, Steady, Go! *are (from left) Hilton Valentine, Alan Price, Eric Burdon, John Steel, Chas Chandler.*

BLUES REBORN (AND IN ENGLAND TOO)

Blues had its roots in black America of the deep South. But the spirit of the music was so potent that it resurfaced spectacularly throughout the rock era, with white musicians contributing as impressively as their black colleagues.

COMING TOGETHER – FOR A WHILE

Like jazz groups, blues bands are more a flexible collection of individuals than the usually more fixed 'group', typical of pop. The Yardbirds were formed in London in 1961, and their line-up over the years included superstar guitarists Eric Clapton (later of Cream), Jeff Beck, and Jimmy Page (later of Led Zeppelin). Keyboard ace John Mayall's Bluesbreakers featured John McVie (later of Fleetwood Mac) on the album *Bluesbreakers with Eric Clapton* (1966). Other members at different times were Peter Green and Mick Fleetwood (also of Fleetwood Mac: p. 20).

SPIRIT OF THE BLUES
Robert Johnson (1911–38) was one of America's great blues artists. His few recordings, especially 'Crossroad Blues', inspired future generations.

CHANGEABLE YARDBIRDS
Some brilliant musicians played with the Yardbirds for a time. Eric Clapton (right) later joined John Mayall's Bluesbreakers, then Cream.

LAUNCH OF A SUPERGROUP
From left, Led Zeppelin's John Paul Jones, Jimmy Page, Robert Plant, John Bonham. They recorded their first album in just two weeks, and soon became the biggest band in the world.

14

SUPREME GUITARIST

Born in Seattle, Jimi Hendrix (1942–70) toured with the Isley Brothers (p. 17) and rock 'n' roll star Little Richard. Then he was spotted by bassist-turned-producer Chas Chandler (p. 13), who brought him to England. The Jimi Hendrix Experience, formed with bass guitarist Noel Redding and drummer Mitch Mitchell, had made Hendrix's dazzling, explosive guitar-playing immortal by the time of his tragically early death.

Over 30 years after his death, many people still consider Jimi Hendrix the finest electric guitarist ever.

'WE ARE THE CREAM'

Cream came together in 1966 and disbanded just two years later. By then a legend had been created by the trio combination of Eric Clapton's virtuoso guitar, Ginger Baker's drumming, and Jack Bruce's harmonica, bass guitar and rasping vocals. Bruce, who was classically trained, once said that Bach's bass lines had greatly influenced his own. Cream's album *Disraeli Gears* (1967) stormed Britain and America. So did the double album *Wheels of Fire* (1968), with its sensational live set, recorded at the Fillmore West in San Francisco.

THE ZEPPELIN IS AIRBORNE

In 1968, Jimmy Page formed the New Yardbirds with bassist and keyboard-player John Paul Jones. With vocalist Robert Plant and drummer John Bonham on board, they renamed themselves, and recorded *Led Zeppelin*. It was one of the most successful first albums ever, and launched a blues and heavy rock style that would dominate the Seventies.

ULTIMATE THREESOME

Jack Bruce (left), Ginger Baker (centre) and Eric Clapton performed as a trio of equals, whose playing was at its most exciting when each one was fighting the others for the lead.

15

AMERICA: SOUL AND FUNK

Like blues and jazz, soul is as much about a musical state of mind as about a particular style. It first surfaced in the Fifties, as a type of jazz reflecting the influence of black gospel music (which itself has roots in hymns and spirituals).

STAX AND MOTOWN

By the Sixties, soul had come to encompass many kinds of black music-making, where elements of gospel rubbed shoulders with rhythm-and-blues. Soul also came to be seen as the unofficial musical voice of America's civil rights movement. Its success was fuelled by the 'house styles' of two dominant record labels. Tamla Motown was presided over by producer Berry Gordy Jnr in northern Detroit. Stax, in southern Memphis, was the empire of producer and singer Otis Redding (1941–67).

MOTOWN MEGASTARS
Diana Ross (centre) led The Supremes to a string of hits, including 'Baby Love' (1964) and 'You Keep Me Hangin' On' (1966).

MOVER AND SHAKER
Besides being a leading soul singer, Otis Redding was the key producer, talent scout and songwriter for Stax Records before his death in an aeroplane crash. His own albums included Otis Blue and The Soul Album (both 1966).

16

A HERO AND A HEROINE

The gritty, super-powerful vocals of James Brown (born 1933) made him a star not just of soul, but of its overlap with funk. This was a movement which in the Fifties had set about putting raw rhythmic energy back into the 'cool' world of much jazz and bebop. Brown now did the same in soul. Aretha Franklin (born 1942) sang with a blend of passion and vocal acrobatics that related more to gospel. She did so in a way that made her the undisputed Queen of Soul.

GODFATHER OF SOUL
James Brown opened up explosive new territory with his powerful, rhythm-based vocal style, as in 'Let Yourself Go' and 'Cold Sweat' (both 1967) and 'Say it Loud – I'm Black and I'm Proud' (1968).

STEVIE WONDER
Blind from birth, Steveland Morris Judkins (born 1950) was a fluent pianist, harmonica-player and drummer by the age of ten. Signed by Motown in 1962 and billed as Little Stevie Wonder, he quickly became one of soul's biggest stars, co-writing and singing some of his own songs, besides performing others such as 'Blowin' in the Wind' by Bob Dylan (p. 18).

Wonder's first album was called The 12 Year Old Genius.

MORE SOUL STARS

Marvin Gaye (1939–84) was a singer-songwriter as gifted and versatile as soul has produced, able to bring jazz elements into a broad musical spectrum ranging from gospel to funk. Diana Ross (born 1944) and her all-female group the Supremes also built up a huge following. The Isley Brothers enthusiastically mixed soul and rhythm-and-blues: 'Twist and Shout' (1962) became a huge hit when the Beatles took it up the next year.

SOULFUL SINGER
Aretha Franklin made her name with a sequence of recordings that contain some of the finest soul singing ever, including 'Respect' (written by Otis Redding), 'Chain of Fools' (both 1967), 'Ain't No Way' and 'The House that Jack Built' (both 1968).

AMERICA: SINGERS AND SONGWRITERS

The age of freedom and resistance, real or imagined, produced musicians who could give voice to the dreams and desires of the new 'liberated' generation. They were the wandering minstrels of their time.

THE TROUBADOUR: BOB DYLAN

Bob Dylan (born 1941) quickly made his name as the leading folk singer of his generation. He wrote his own songs, often to complex and bitter lyrics with a sharp political slant, and he used electric as well as acoustic guitar. *Highway 61 Revisited* (1965) is a classic album of its period. After a motorcycle accident in 1966, Dylan's tone changed. *John Wesley Harding* (1968) shows the gentler influence of country music, with many references to the Bible.

Simon (left) and Garfunkel first met at school.

SIMON AND GARFUNKEL

The influence of 1950s stars the Everly Brothers can be heard in the close-harmony duetting of singer-songwriter-guitarist Paul Simon and vocalist Art Garfunkel (both born 1941), whose career as a folk-rock phenomenon took off with 'The Sound of Silence' (1966). Their album *Parsley, Sage, Rosemary and Thyme* (1966) became the basis for Simon's film score for *The Graduate* (1968). *Bookends* (1968) was their Sixties masterpiece.

CHALLENGING THE STATUS QUO
Bob Dylan and Joan Baez both held a strongly anti-establishment viewpoint. Here they sing together at the 1963 Newport Folk Festival.

VOICES OF THEIR TIME

With her strongly anti-establishment political views, Joan Baez (born 1941) came to symbolize the civil rights movement, especially from the standpoint of its white supporters. Janis Joplin (1943–70) developed spectacularly from her roots as a folk and blues singer, spending months at the top of the American charts before and after her early death.

ARTIST OF EXTREMES
The dark, tortured side of the blues can be heard in Janis Joplin's albums Cheap Thrills *(1968) and* Pearl *(released in 1971, just months after her death).*

CALIFORNIA DREAMING

Formed in 1961 in Los Angeles, the Beach Boys summed up the early-Sixties Californian dream of sun, surfing, and cruising about in huge cars. Their first hit was 'Surfin' Safari' (1962). Brian Wilson, one of three brothers in the group, emerged as a talented songwriter. The Byrds, another LA band, came up with a new sound in their dreamy, shimmering version of Dylan's 'Mr Tambourine Man' in 1965. The line-up included David Crosby, who in 1968 formed a trio with two other guitarist-songwriters, Stephen Stills and Graham Nash.

CLEAN-CUT (AT FIRST)
By the mid-Sixties the Beach Boys were developing a more experimental style of rock. Pet Sounds *(1966) influenced the Beatles'* Sergeant Pepper's Lonely Hearts Club Band.

FRESH SOUNDS
The Byrds' style, based on folk and country rather than rock, also influenced the Beatles, in Rubber Soul *and* Revolver.

ROCK GOES COSMIC

As technology – particularly recording technology – raced ahead, rock looked to explore the further shores of musical imagination. One way of doing this was to experiment with the forms and resources of classical music.

ROCK MEETS CLASSICAL

Days of Future Passed (1968) by the Moody Blues linked the group's rock numbers with interludes for symphony orchestra. London's The Who were already notorious as England's wildest rhythm-and-blues band when their lead guitarist, Pete Townshend, created his rock opera, *Tommy*, in 1969. America's Frank Zappa brought together influences as wide as rhythm-and-blues and the classical modernism of Stravinsky and Varèse. Zappa's *Lumpy Gravy* (1968) and *Uncle Meat* (1969) were two of the startling results.

FLEETWOOD MAC IS LAUNCHED

In 1969, Fleetwood Mac was based around Mick Fleetwood (drums), Peter Green (guitar and vocals) and John McVie (bass guitar), all one-time members of John Mayall's band (p. 14). They scored their first major hit single with 'Albatross'. The futuristic sound-world of London's Pink Floyd produced *Piper at the Gates of Dawn* (1967). This was their only album with the brilliant songwriter Syd Barrett, who left the band soon after.

PATH TO THE FUTURE
Pink Floyd were early users of light shows in their stage act. Clockwise from top left: Roger Waters (bass guitar and vocals), Syd Barrett (guitar), Rick Wright (keyboards), Nick Mason (drums).

20

ROCK OPERA

Pete Townshend's Tommy *explored the surrounding world from the viewpoint of a 'deaf, dumb and blind boy'. The title role was sung by The Who's lead singer, Roger Daltrey (left).* Tommy *was later turned into a film (starring Daltrey) and a successful stage musical.*

ROCK AND CLASSICAL COME TOGETHER

The newly formed Deep Purple had everyone surprised, and many people impressed, by the ambitious rock-and-classical 'crossover' of Concerto for Group and Orchestra (1969). This was written by their classically trained keyboard player Jon Lord. Malcolm Arnold (p. 8) scored the orchestral accompaniment and conducted the work at London's 1969 Promenade Concerts.

Arnold (conducting) rehearses the Concerto by Lord (on keyboards).

EXOTIC WORLDS

Folk, blues and far-out experiment came together in the music of Jefferson Airplane. Female lead singers in Sixties rock bands were quite rare, but Grace Slick's vocals and songwriting graced the group's albums *Surrealistic Pillow* (1967) and *Crown of Creation* (1968). *Anthem of the Sun* (1968) and *Aoxomoxoa* (1969) by the Grateful Dead, another Californian band, featured daring, avant-garde musical adventures by keyboard player Tom Constanten, an ex-pupil of Berio (p. 26), Boulez and Stockhausen (pp. 6–7).

DARK JOURNEY

Formed in Los Angeles in 1965, the Doors were led on their psychedelic musical voyage by singer-songwriter Jim Morrison (above), who died in 1971.

CITY OF DREAMS

The Haight Ashbury district of San Francisco was where the hippie and 'flower power' movements started out. Pictured here in their native city are the Grateful Dead, one of rock's longest-lived groups. Surviving members of the band still play today.

JAZZ IN THE SIXTIES

Jazz in the Sixties mirrored the increasingly exotic experiments of rock. Leading jazz players explored new musical frontiers, building on the complex, improvised freedoms of bebop and the radical sounds of the classical avant-garde.

ORNETTE COLEMAN: FREEFORM JAZZ

Alto and tenor saxophonist Ornette Coleman (born 1930) opened up a new world of jazz performance, playing in a quartet without a piano or guitar. In *This is Our Music* and *Free Jazz* (both 1960), saxes, trumpet, bass and drums were all melodic soloists at the same time, without a supporting harmonic accompaniment.

AN ADVENTUROUS TALENT

John Coltrane (1926–67) was already a star from his days of playing tenor sax in groups with Dizzy Gillespie (1917–93) and Miles Davis (1926–91). He now took 'hard bop' jazz into the advanced harmonic world of the avant-garde, with elaborate improvization sessions that became known as 'sheets of sound'. These were partly inspired by Coltrane's interest in eastern and African music, while his religious beliefs were vividly expressed in his legendary album *A Love Supreme* (1965).

PUSHING BACK THE BOUNDARIES
John Coltrane anticipated the 'fusion' jazz of the 1970s by welcoming the influence of musicians from other cultures.

22

ROLAND KIRK

Blind almost from birth, Rahsaan Roland Kirk (1936–77) mastered the art of playing three different kinds of saxophone at once: tenor, and two unusual alto and soprano types called stritchophone and manzello. The idea had come to him in a dream. Kirk worked out a way of fingering all three together, to play a three-part harmony whose sound was unique.

The name 'Rahsaan' also came to Roland Kirk in a dream.

THE MASTERS: MILES DAVIS, ART BLAKEY

In the late Sixties Miles Davis, too, began to explore complex areas of jazz-rock fusion. He played on trumpet and flugelhorn alongside pianists Chick Corea (born 1941), Herbie Hancock (born 1940) and Keith Jarrett (born 1945), guitarist John McLaughlin (born 1942), and sometimes also rock and Indian musicians, in albums such as *In a Silent Way* (1969). Many present and future stars, including Corea and Jarrett, also worked with the 'hard bop' Jazz Messengers, led by virtuoso drummer Art Blakey (1919–90).

LEGENDARY DRUMMER
Art Blakey brilliantly took his drumming style, formed during the swing era, into the new age of bebop and progressive jazz. His finest albums include Free For All *(1965) and* Kyoto *(1968).*

FROM BLUES TO JAZZ
Yorkshire-born guitarist John McLaughlin played rhythm-and-blues with Eric Clapton, Ginger Baker and others before working in New York, contributing to Miles Davis's In a Silent Way.

AMERICA: STRAVINSKY TO CAGE

America's classical composers were led by a gifted older generation, whose styles varied as much as life on the continent itself. The Russian-born Igor Stravinsky (1882–1971), now an American citizen, was their remarkable figurehead.

CARTER: ADVANCED ENERGY

Elliott Carter (born 1908) had developed a style of composing as complex as the European avant-garde's, but his music's tone was different from theirs. Carter's Double Concerto for Harpsichord, Piano and Two Chamber Orchestras (1961), Piano Concerto (1965) and Concerto for Orchestra (1969) were all highly dramatic works in a quite traditional sense. Beethoven would have recognized the underlying idea, if not the style.

STILL THE GREATEST

Most composers mellow as they age. Stravinsky, on the contrary, now composed the most exploratory music of his life, brilliantly adapting the serial technique pioneered by Arnold Schoenberg (1874–1951) to his own musical style. Two of Stravinsky's last works, *A Sermon, a Narrative and a Prayer* (1961) and *Requiem Canticles* (1966), are among the finest he ever wrote.

Stravinsky conducting, drawn by Milein Cosman

MUSICAL EXPLORER
Elliott Carter (right) had by now evolved the intricate composing technique of 'metric modulation', where the music's momentum is controlled by different layers of music that are performed simultaneously, some of them starting slowly and accelerating while other, quicker ones slow down.

CAGE: QUIET REBELLION

For many decades John Cage (1912–92) had been exploring the outer reaches of what western classical music could seem to include: his famous *4′33″* (1952) is for a totally silent piano and/or any other group of performers. Cage found a connection between eastern ways of thought, such as Zen Buddhism, and the aleatory, 'chance' devices of his own music. Examples of these 'happenings' (which in their way are precisely organized) are *Cartridge Music* (1960), based on the random amplified scratchings of an LP stylus, and *HPSCHD* (1969), for harpsichord sounds on computer-manipulated tape.

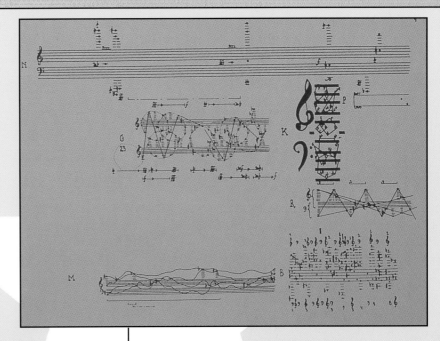

THE PERFORMERS DECIDE
This page from John Cage's Piano Concerto gives the player maximum scope to improvise notes and the order of events within particular musical guidelines.

AMERICAN MASTERS: BERNSTEIN AND COPLAND

At the height of his busy career as a conductor, Leonard Bernstein (1918–90) made time to compose his Judaism-inspired Third Symphony ('Kaddish', 1963) and *Chichester Psalms* (1965). The film of his musical *West Side Story* was released in 1961. Aaron Copland (1900–90) wrote a ballet, *Dance Panels* (1963), relating to his earlier, populist style, and also two orchestral works, *Connotations* (1962) and *Inscape* (1967).

ALL-ROUNDER
Besides his composing, Bernstein also had a spectacular career conducting the New York Philharmonic Orchestra as their first (and so far only) American-born music director.

SENIOR COMPOSER
Aaron Copland (drawn by Milein Cosman) wrote 'advanced' works besides more openly listener-friendly ones.

ITALIAN RADICALS

Beneath its stylish and increasingly prosperous surface, Italy in the Sixties was a nation of increasing conflict between the right-wing parties connected to the Catholic church and the Marxist left. The music of its composers reflected this.

WAYS OF EXPRESSION

Musical radicalism comes out in very different ways. The approach adopted by Luciano Berio (born 1925) was to search out the essence of how music expresses itself in different techniques and styles. Like many of Berio's vocal works, *Epifanie* (Epiphany, 1961), a song-cycle with orchestra, was written for his wife, the American soprano Cathy Berberian. Berio's *Sinfonia* (1969) was composed for the popular Swingle Singers as soloists with the orchestra. It quotes music by Mahler, Schoenberg and other composers within the context of Berio's own.

REBEL WITH A CAUSE

For Luigi Nono (1924–90), radical politics related to his own individual development of Schoenberg's serial method. At the première of his one-act opera *Intolleranza 1960* (Intolerance 1960) in Venice, there were street demonstrations between left- and right-wing groups. *Per Bastiana Tai-Yang Cheng* (For Bastiana [Nono's daughter] the East is Red, 1967), for orchestra and electronic tape, was Nono's salute to Communist China.

Luigi Nono, for whom music and message were as one.

BERIO'S IDEAL SINGER

Cathy Berberian (1925–83), married to Berio from 1950 to 1966, was trained in dance and mime besides singing, and excelled in avant-garde music. Berio composed several works for her, including Circles *(1960) for soprano, harp and percussion and* Sequenza III *(1966) for solo voice.*

26

AN ANCIENT STORY RE-TOLD

Luigi Dallapiccola (1904–75) spent most of the decade working on his crowning masterpiece, the large-scale opera *Ulisse* (Ulysses: the Roman name for the Ancient Greek hero, Odysseus). Completed in 1968, this tells the story of Homer's *Odyssey*. In its epilogue, Dallapiccola adds a Christian message: Ulysses, the perpetual wanderer, first becomes aware of God. The music's tone is mostly quiet, but with great power behind it.

AN AVANT-GARDIST WITH CHARM

Bruno Maderna (1920–73) was famous as a conductor, often of avant-garde works by his contemporaries, but he was also a fine composer. Like Berio, Nono and Dallapiccola, he was able to blend advanced techniques with attractive sounds. Two of Maderna's three Oboe Concertos were composed in 1962 and 1967. *Quadrivium* (1969), for percussion quartet and orchestra, is more radical music.

EASTERN EUROPE: REPRESSION AND RESISTANCE

ELife in the Soviet Union and eastern Europe was very different from that in the democracies of the west. Individual freedoms, including cultural freedoms, were controlled and often sharply restricted by their Communist governments.

WANDERING MINSTRELS
Polish hippies try hitching a lift outside the capital, Warsaw. The notice says: 'Driver, help the child'.

SAME AGAIN (ALMOST)
Soviet dictator Stalin's successor, Nikita Krushchev, relaxed the Communists' rule of eastern Europe, but not by much.

MUSIC IN POLAND: NEW POSSIBILITIES

Most countries in eastern Europe insisted that music should serve the cause of 'socialist realism'. This meant composing as conservatively as possible. Poland's authorities, however, took a different view, and responded to the rise of the western avant-garde by giving their own composers scope to compete with it. Radical modernism, far from being repressed, was suddenly a requirement.

SHOSTAKOVICH DOESN'T COMPROMISE

The earlier years of Stalinist persecution had permanently marked Dmitri Shostakovich (1906–75). His Thirteenth Symphony (1962) was a setting of texts by the poet Yevgeny Yevtushenko criticising aspects of Soviet Russia, especially its anti-semitism. The Soviet authorities angrily postponed its first performance. The more private tone of Shostakovich's string quartets (Nos. 8 to 12, 1960–68) is dark and haunted.

A composer who stayed true to himself.

FROM FOLK MUSIC TO ALEATORIC ADVENTURE

When the official line changed in Poland, Witold Lutoslawski (1913–94), whose early style related to that of Hungary's Béla Bartók (1881–1945), responded with *Venetian Games* (1961) for orchestra. This contrasted sections constructed in 'aleatoric' style, where the rhythms of the individual instruments are free, with other sections where they are strict. In his String Quartet (1964) and *Livre pour Orchestre* (Book for Orchestra, 1968), Lutoslawski took this idea further.

DELAYED FAME
Lutoslawski had a major international success with Three Poems of Henri Michaux *(1963) for chorus, wind instruments and percussion.*

MODERNIST MEMORIAL
Penderecki dedicated his choral Dies Irae *(1967) to the victims of Auschwitz concentration camp, where the work's first performance took place.*

A CHRISTIAN MODERNIST

The style of Krzysztof Penderecki (born 1933) was bolder, exploring extremes of high and low register in dense slabs and clusters of choral and orchestral sound. Penderecki's *Threnody for the Victims of Hiroshima* (1960) for 52 solo strings was performed by orchestras all over the world. His large-scale, choral *St Luke Passion* (1965) contrasted this interest in avant-garde sounds with a more traditional, chant-based style to tell the story of Christ's crucifixion and death.

GLOSSARY

ALEATORY 'Chance music', whose order – notes, sections, or even whole movements – is left to the performers to decide, sometimes during the performance itself.

ATONAL Music which is not in a conventional key.

AVANT-GARDE An artistic movement more challenging than conventional styles.

BEBOP (or Bop) A type of jazz involving a complex mix of melody, harmony and rhythm.

CHAMBER MUSIC For a group of solo players.

CONCERTO A work with one or more solo instruments and an orchestra.

FLUGELHORN A brass instrument with the full, rounded sound of the bugle, but with the keyed mechanism of the trumpet.

HARD BOP A type of modern jazz, which is derived from bebop, but is generally faster and more aggressive.

HARPSICHORD A keyboard instrument whose strings are plucked by quills, making a twanging sound.

MODERNIST Music that sounds modern compared to what had come before.

ORATORIO A large-scale setting of a text on a religious subject.

QUARTET/STRING QUARTET A work for four instruments; also the group that plays them. A string quartet consists of two violins, viola and cello.

SERIALISM A way of ordering the notes in modernist music.

SINFONIA The Italian word for 'symphony'.

SYMPHONY Traditionally, an orchestral work in four separate movements.

TENOR A middling-high male voice – compared to alto and soprano, the lower and higher types of female voice. Also a particular size of saxophone.

TROUBADOUR A singer-songwriter in medieval France and Italy, who travelled widely and often won great fame.

VARIATIONS A musical form where an idea is at first stated and then 'varied' several times over, by decorating the melody, elaborating the harmony, or a combination of both methods.

30

WORLD EVENTS

- John F. Kennedy elected US President
- American spy plane downed over Russia

- The Berlin Wall is raised
- First man in space: Soviet Yuri Gagarin

- Cuban missile crisis almost leads to a Third World War

- President Kennedy assassinated
- Martin Luther King fights for civil rights

- Palestinian Liberation Organization created

- America escalates its involvement in Vietnam War

- Soviet Union lands unmanned spacecraft on the Moon

- Six Day War between Israel and surrounding Arab countries

- Anti-government riots in Europe and America

- American astronauts land on the Moon
- British troops deployed in Ulster

TIMELINE

MUSICAL EVENTS	THE ARTS	FAMOUS MUSICIANS	MUSICAL WORKS
•The 'twist' becomes a dance craze that sweeps the world	•Alfred Hitchcock's film Psycho released •Stanley Kubrick's film Spartacus	•Death of Leonard Warren, American baritone singer	•Walton's Second Symphony •Lerner and Loewe's musical Camelot
•'Biggest Show of Stars' tour of US with Fats Domino, Chubby Checker, The Drifters	•Russian dancer Rudolf Nureyev defects to the west	•Birth of Wynton Marsalis, jazz trumpeter	•Stravinsky's A Sermon, a Narrative and a Prayer •Britten's War Requiem
•The Beatles offered a recording contract •Première of Tippett's opera King Priam	•Death of film star Marilyn Monroe •David Lean's film Lawrence of Arabia	•Birth of Garth Brooks, country and western singer	•Shostakovich's Thirteenth Symphony 'Babiy Yar'
•Joan Baez and Bob Dylan appear at Newport Folk Festival	•Neil Simon's play Barefoot in the Park •James Bond film From Russia with Love	•Deaths of Paul Hindemith, Francis Poulenc and Edith Piaf, French popular singer	•Messiaen's Colours of the Celestial City •The Beatles' Please Please Me album
•UK – Richmond Jazz and Blues Festival stars the Rolling Stones	•Arthur Miller's play After the Fall •Peter Sellers stars in film Doctor Strangelove	•The Byrds are formed in Los Angeles •Topol stars in Fiddler on the Roof	•Stockhausen's Momente (Moments) •My Fair Lady soundtrack
•The Rolling Stones' '(I Can't Get No) Satisfaction' sweeps Britain and America	•Michael Caine stars in film The Ipcress File •Death of T.S. Eliot, American born poet	•Death of Nat 'King' Cole, American jazz singer and pianist	•The Who's 'My Generation' •John Coltrane's A Love Supreme album
•The Beach Boys' Pet Sounds album features early electronic instruments	•Floods destroy many works of art in Florence •Start of The Monkees TV show in America	•Birth of Cecilia Bartoli, Italian mezzo-soprano •The Beatles retire from touring	•Stravinsky's Requiem Canticles •Bob Dylan's Blonde on Blonde album
•BBC Radio 1 launched •June – Monterey pop festival, California	•Mike Nichols's film The Graduate stars Dustin Hoffman	•Genesis is formed at Charterhouse school, England •Death of John Coltrane	•Copland's Inscape •The Beatles' Sergeant Pepper's Lonely Hearts Club Band
•First albums from Led Zeppelin, Deep Purple, Fleetwood Mac and Jethro Tull	•American TV launch of the Dick Cavett Show •Stanley Kubrick's film 2001: A Space Odyssey	•Syd Barrett quits Pink Floyd •Cream splits up	•Stockhausen's Stimmung (Tuning and/or Mood) •The Rolling Stones' Beggars Banquet album
•450,000 gather at Woodstock rock festival in New York State	•British TV: first season of Monty Python's Flying Circus	•The Rolling Stones' Brian Jones dies •Death of saxophonist Coleman Hawkins	•Shostakovich's Fourteenth Symphony •Frank Sinatra's My Way album

INDEX